W9-BBN-014

CPS-Morrill School Library

34880 00010365 0

Chancellor, Deborah   SP 629.04 CHA
Viajes por tierra

DATE DUE

SP
629.04   Chancellor, Deborah
CHA   Viajes por tierra

Morrill School Library
Chicago Public Schools
6011 S. Rockwell
Chicago, IL 60629

SP
629.04
Cha

VIAJES
POR TIERRA

DEBORAH CHANCELLOR

TWO CAN

PRINCETON • LONDON

Cómo usar este libro

Referencias cruzadas
Busca las páginas que se citan en la parte superior de las páginas de la izquierda para saber más de cada tema.

Glosario
Las palabras de difícil significado se explican en el glosario que encontrarás al final del libro. Estas palabras aparecen en negritas a lo largo de todo el texto.

Índice
Al final del libro encontrarás el índice, que relaciona por orden alfabético la mayoría de las palabras que aparecen en el texto. Localiza en el índice la palabra de tu interés y ¡verás en qué página aparece la palabra!

Curiosidades
En este apartado encontrarás datos de interés sobre otros asuntos relacionados con el tema.

Haz la prueba
Estas burbujas te permiten poner en práctica algunas de las ideas de este libro. Así podrás comprobar si esas ideas funcionan.

Rincón bilingüe
Aquí encontrarás las palabras clave de cada tema, así como frases y preguntas relacionadas con el mismo. ¿Puedes contestar las preguntas? Verás también las **palabras clave en inglés**, junto con su **pronunciación inglesa**. Practica en inglés las palabras que aparecen en negrita dentro de las frases y preguntas.

Contenido

Fuerza animal

Antiguamente, el único modo de viajar era a pie y la gente utilizaba los animales para transportar **cargas** y cabalgar. Viajar fue más fácil cuando los antiguos sumerios inventaron la rueda. Con ella, los animales pudieron arrastrar carretas que transportaban gente y cargamentos. Hoy, en muchos sitios, los animales son todavía un medio de transporte y de trabajo.

La invención de la rueda

Las primeras ruedas eran de madera, sólidas y pesadas, y giraban lentamente. Con el tiempo, se construyeron ruedas más ligeras que giraban más rápido. Las ruedas con **radios** pesan mucho menos, y son tan sólidas y fuertes como las primeras.

La domesticación de los animales

Para que los animales transporten **cargas** y gente deben ser domesticados. El animal que arrastra una carreta tiene que aprender a llevar un arnés.

▲ Estos caballos arrastran una diligencia llena de pasajeros y su equipaje.

▼ Las llamas, con sus pezuñas hendidas, pueden mantener el equilibrio al ascender por terrenos pedregosos.

Animales de trabajo

En todo el mundo, la gente utiliza a los animales para realizar trabajos pesados. Algunos, como los elefantes, pueden mover cargas pesadas que la gente no puede mover. Otros, las llamas y los camellos, pueden subir a sitios adonde los carros y los camiones no pueden llegar.

Rincón Bilingüe

auto · car · *car*
camello · camel · *quémel*
cargas · baggage · *béguech*
elefante · elephant · *élefant*
llama · llama · *lama*
ruedas · wheels · *uíls*
trabajo · work · *uórk*
viaje · travel · *trável*

El **elefante** puede mover **cargas** muy pesadas. ¿Por qué son importantes las **ruedas**?

▲ Estos elefantes han sido amaestrados en Tailandia para mover pesados troncos con sus colmillos.

véase: Motocicletas, pág. 8

Bicicletas

Las bicicletas son máquinas sencillas que tienen dos ruedas. La gente las mueve girando los pedales con sus pies. Son baratas y no **contaminan** porque no tienen motor. En todo el mundo, niños y adultos viajan en bicicleta. Son también útiles porque se pueden manejar por los lugares por donde no pueden ir los coches.

Cambiar a una marcha más baja, le permite pedalear en las cuestas hacia arriba.

Con los manillares, el ciclista guía la bicicleta y mantiene el equilibrio.

▲ Este ciclista está haciendo acrobacias, pero se ha puesto ropa acolchada, casco y lentes de seguridad por si se cae.

Los frenos rozan contra la rueda para aminorar la marcha.

El estadounidense Steve Roberts inventó una bicicleta muy rara. Lleva a bordo cuatro computadoras y una nevera que funcionan por los rayos solares.

Bicicletas de alquiler

En algunos países, se utilizan los rickshaw para desplazarse. Esta variedad de bicicletas suele tener tres ruedas, y las personas que las utilizan le pagan al conductor para que las transporte.

▲ Los rickshaw de tres ruedas son de fácil manejo. También transportan **cargas**.

La cadena transmite impulso a la rueda trasera y hace que gire.

*Con la superficie rugosa, o **rodadura**, las llantas se agarran al suelo.*

Los pedales están conectados a la rueda trasera con la cadena.

Rincón Bilingüe

bicicleta · bicycle · *báissiquel*
casco · helmet · *gélmet*
ciclista · bicyclist · *báissiclist*
fácil · easy · *íisi*

máquina · machine · *mashín*
neumático · tire · *táiar*
pedal · pedal · *pédal*
potencia · power · *páuer*

Tú eres el motor de tu **bicicleta**.
No debes montar en **bicicleta** sin usar el **casco** protector.
Los **ciclistas** no contaminan el aire.

véase: Bicicletas, pág. 6

Motocicletas

La motocicleta se parece a la bicicleta pero se mueve impulsada por un **motor**. Es más pesada y más rápida que la bicicleta. La primera motocicleta se construyó en Alemania en 1885, y alcanzaba una velocidad de 12 km por hora. Hoy, las motocicletas alcanzan velocidades mucho más altas. El récord mundial es de 513 km por hora.

CURIOSIDADES

¿Cuántas personas crees que pueden caber en equilibrio en una motocicleta? En 1987, en New South Wales, Australia, 47 personas consiguieron viajar en una sola moto.

El casco protege la cabeza del moticiclista en caso de accidente...................

El escudo de plástico duro protege del viento al motociclista....................

Las ropas de cuero protegen el cuerpo y lo mantienen caliente. ....

Agarre

Cuando la moto se mueve, las **rodaduras** de la llanta originan una **fricción** entre la llanta y el suelo. La fricción permite que la llanta se agarre al suelo.

▼ Las motocicletas de montaña, que corren en todo tipo de terreno, se usan para practicar motocross.

HAZ LA PRUEBA

*Toma un pequeño bloque de madera y ponle papel de lija a uno de sus lados. Primero desliza el bloque por una pendiente con el lado liso hacia abajo. Después deslizalo por el lado áspero. El lado áspero será más lento por la **fricción**.*

Motos de montaña

Algunas motos no se fabrican para carreteras. Las motos de montaña corren a campo traviesa, incluso por caminos que no son de tierra. También atraviesan riachuelos y escalan colinas.

*Las **rodaduras** de las llantas permiten mayor agarre.*

Rincón Bilingüe

colina · hill · *jil*
corriente · stream · *strím*
escudo · shield · *shild*
fricción · friction · *fricshion*

fuerte · strong · *strong*
motor · engine · *énchin*
plástico · plastic · *plástic*
rápido · fast · *fast*

La **motocicleta** puede desplazarse muy rápidamente.
¿Tiene **motor** la **motocicleta**?
¿Cómo actúa la **fricción**?

véase: Motocicletas, pág. 8; Autobuses y tranvías, pág. 12

Automóviles

Una de las maneras más fáciles y rápidas de viajar es con el auto. Casi todos los autos tienen motores de gasolina. Dentro del **motor**, ésta se quema para producir **energía**, que empuja al auto. El primer auto con motor de gasolina se construyó en 1885, por el alemán Karl Benz. Tenía tres ruedas, en vez de cuatro, y corría a unos 13 km por hora.

En casi todos los autos, el motor está delante, debajo del capó.

De noche, los conductores encienden los faros para ver la carretera delante de ellos. Los intermitentes indican a otros conductores si el coche va a girar a la derecha o a la izquierda.

Autos aerodinámicos

Los *ingenieros* intentan diseñar autos cada vez más *aerodinámicos*, de forma lisa y plana. Éstos circulan más rápido, pues el aire se mueve más fácilmente sobre ellos. Los que no son aerodinámicos gastan más gasolina.

El volante sirve para girar el auto.

Los cinturones protegen a los conductores y pasajeros en un accidente.

Velocidad

El auto de carreras tiene forma **aerodinámica** que le permite viajar a gran velocidad.

◀ **Durante las carreras, los mecánicos cambian rápidamente las ruedas y llenan los depósitos.**

Evitar el tráfico

Hoy día circulan muchos más autos que nunca. En las grandes ciudades, como México DF, hay a veces tantos autos en una calle que no pueden avanzar y se forman embotellamientos.

De noche, las luces traseras permiten que el coche de atrás vea al que va delante.

Rincón Bilingüe

auto · car · *car*
carretera · road · *róud*
frenos · brakes · *bréics*
asiento · seat · *síit*
gasolina · gasoline · *gasolin*
volante · steering wheel · *stíring uíil*
energía · energy · *énerchi*
cinturón de seguridad · seat belt · *sit belt*

Muchas ciudades están repletas de **autos**. La mayoría de los **autos** usan **gasolina**.

véase: Automóviles, pág. 10

Autobuses y tranvías

Si todo el mundo viajara en autobús y no en auto, habría menos tráfico en las calles. Los autobuses transportan a mucha gente por la misma **ruta**. Son ideales para los desplazamientos cortos y para viajar largas distancias. Consumen menos **combustible** que el que se utilizaría con automóviles.

Transporte público

En las ciudades hay redes de autobuses para cuyo uso la gente paga una tarifa. Es un tipo de transporte público. Cada autobús sigue una **ruta** distinta, que suele ir señalada con un número. La gente espera en las paradas. Cuando se sube, compra un ticket y con él paga su viaje.

▼ Este autobús recorre una ruta en Londres, Inglaterra. Tiene dos **plataformas** y transporta unas 90 personas.

Viajar a grandes distancias

Otros **vehículos** grandes, los autocares, recorren grandes distancias, desde una ciudad a otra. Están diseñados para que el viaje sea confortable. Tienen asientos cómodos, baños e, incluso, pantallas de video y cine.

Rincón Bilingüe

autobús · bus · *bos*
cable · cable · *quéibel*
combustible · fuel · *fiúel*
electricidad · electricity · *electríssiti*
mapa · map · *map*
ruta · route · *rut*
tranvías · trams · *trams*
viaje · journey · *chóurnei*

Los viajes en **autobús** pueden ser divertidos. ¿Has montado alguna vez en un **tranvía**?

◀ Los autobuses en muchos países están decorados de vistosos colores. Casi siempre van muy llenos.

Tranvías

Muchas ciudades tienen tranvías y autobuses. Los tranvías circulan por rieles colocados en las calles. Son un excelente tipo de transporte porque no **contaminan**.

Cómo funcionan

Los tranvías se mueven por electricidad. Tienen un dispositivo, el pantógrafo, en el techo, que recoge electricidad de los cables instalados en lo alto de las calles.

pantógrafo

cables

CURIOSIDADES

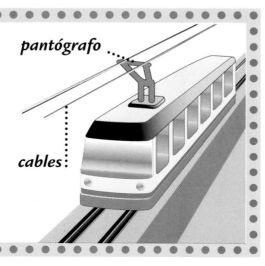

Caracas

La **ruta** más larga del mundo en autobús va desde Caracas, Venezuela hasta Buenos Aires, Argentina. Incluidas las paradas, el viaje dura casi nueve días.

Buenos Aires

véase: Otros vehículos, pág. 16

Camiones de carga

Los camiones son grandes **vehículos** que transportan objetos pesados por carretera. Normalmente, es la manera más barata de mover **cargas** pesadas. Hay diferentes tipos de esta clase de transporte. Los camiones refrigeradores, por ejemplo, transportan alimentos congelados. Poseen equipos especiales que mantienen en hielo los alimentos.

Motores potentes

Los camiones necesitan **motores** potentes para sus pesadas **cargas**. Un capó especial sobre la cabina, el deflector de aire, hace que el camión sea más **aerodinámico**. Esto significa que gasta menos **combustible**.

▼ Antes de comenzar el viaje, los mecánicos comprueban que el motor y las ruedas estén en perfecto estado.

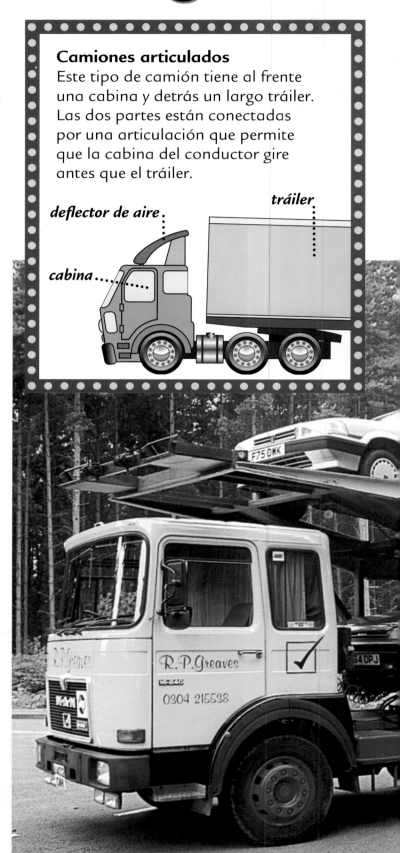

Camiones articulados

Este tipo de camión tiene al frente una cabina y detrás un largo tráiler. Las dos partes están conectadas por una articulación que permite que la cabina del conductor gire antes que el tráiler.

deflector de aire

cabina

tráiler

▲ En Australia, enormes camiones, llamados trenes de carretera, pueden transportar el contenido de tres tráilers juntos.

Rincón Bilingüe

aerodinámico · aerodynamic · *aéro-dainámic*
cabina · cab · *kab*
camiones · trucks · *troks*
carga · load · *lóud*
carretera · road · *róud*
chofer · driver · *dráiver*
mecánico · mechanic · *mekánik*
tráiler · trailer · *tréiler*

¿Cuál es el trabajo del **mecánico** de **camiones**?
¿Viaja el chofer en el **tráiler** o en la **cabina**?

▼ Los transportadores de coches son grandes camiones de varias **plataformas** que cargan muchos coches.

Conducción cómoda

La parte delantera de los camiones de carga es la cabina, donde se sienta el conductor. Tiene que ser muy confortable porque el conductor recorre grandes distancias. Las cabinas tienen camas detrás de los asientos para que el conductor pueda descansar.

Cargas líquidas

Los camiones cisterna se construyen especialmente para transportar líquidos cómo aceite o leche. El tráiler debe estar perfectamente sellado para que no se derrame su carga. Su interior se divide en secciones separadas para evitar que el líquido chapotee.

véase: Camiones de carga, pág. 14

Otros vehículos

Hay varios tipos de camiones de trabajo y realizan diferentes cometidos. Los camiones recogedores de basura retiran ésta de las casas. Las excavadoras limpian el suelo. Los constructores y los agricultores, entre otros, utilizan estos camiones para facilitar el trabajo.

El camión grúa sirve para levantar grandes pesos.

El tambor de la mezcladora de cemento mezcla arena, cemento y agua para obtener concreto.

CURIOSIDADES

Las llantas que se fabrican para enormes camiones de volteo tienen una altura de 3 m, casi el doble de la estatura de una persona mayor.

El bulldozer utiliza su gran pala para sacar gran cantidad de tierra y piedras.

Sitio de construcción
En estos sitios los camiones de trabajo se usan para tirar abajo las viejas construcciones, para mover pilotes y para mezclar cemento; circulan en terreno pedregoso gracias a sus grandes y fuertes llantas.

Los camiones de volteo llevan la tierra a otro lugar. Su tráiler es móvil, para poder vaciar la tierra.

16

En la granja

Antes, la gente y los animales tenían que trabajar duramente en el campo. Hoy, los tractores y las segadoras combinadas facilitan ese trabajo. Éste se realiza con menor esfuerzo y mucho más rápidamente.

◀ **La segadora combinada realiza el trabajo de varias personas. Corta la planta y separa el grano de la paja.**

...El brazo móvil de la excavadora se inclina para sacar tierra y depositarla en el camión de volteo.

Rincón Bilingüe

bulldozer · bulldozer · *buldósser*
cemento · cement · *síment*
concreto · concrete · *concrít*
cosechadora · harvester · *járvester*
basura · garbage · *gárbech*
mezcladora · mixer · *míxer*
piedras · stones · *stóuns*
suelo · soil · *sóil*

¡Qué divertido es manejar un **bulldozer**!
La **mezcladora** de **cemento** es pesada.

véase: Otros vehículos, pág. 16

Emergencias

Cuando se presenta una emergencia, como un accidente o un incendio, acuden para ayudar autos o camiones especiales, y llegan lo más rápidamente posible. Estos **vehículos** están diseñados para realizar diferentes trabajos.

Bombas extinguidoras

Se usan para apagar incendios y rescatar a la gente atrapada en los edificios. Llevan mangueras, escaleras, cubetas y arena. Otras llevan grandes cantidades de agua.

▶ Los bomberos usan también sus largas escaleras para rescatar mascotas.

La escalera del coche de .... bomberos puede llegar hasta la parte más alta de los árboles y edificios.

Los bomberos tienen ...... que ponerse ropas especiales y cascos resistentes para no resultar lesionados.

▲ Los coches de la policía tienen **sirenas** y luces para avisar a los automovilistas que les dejen paso libre.

HAZ LA PRUEBA

Las ambulancias llevan colores vistosos para que sean bien visibles. Intenta saber con esta prueba qué color es más vistoso. Pide a un amigo que se ponga una camiseta verde y, a otro, una camiseta rosa. ¿Cuál se ve mejor desde lejos?

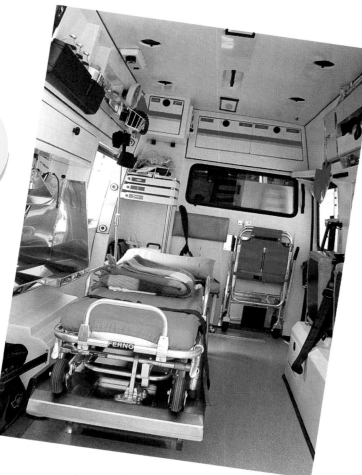

▲ **La ambulancia está diseñada para que la tripulación alcance los instrumentos rápidamente.**

Dentro de una ambulancia

Las ambulancias son como hospitales en pequeño. Dentro llevan medicinas y equipo para salvar la vida. También va a bordo una tripulación, que lleva a la gente en camilla a la ambulancia y la cuida en el camino al hospital.

Controles automáticos a un lado del coche de bomberos sirven para subir o bajar la escalera.

Rincón Bilingüe

accidente · accident · *áccident*
ambulancia · ambulance · *ámbiulans*
coche de bomberos · fire engine · *fáier énchin*
emergencia · emergency · *emérchenssi*
escalera · ladder · *ládder*
fuego · fire · *fáier*
manguera · hose · *jóus*
sirena · siren · *sáiren*

¿Te has subido a un **coche de bomberos**?
¿Por qué tienen **sirenas** las **ambulancias**?

véase: Automóviles, pág. 10

Carreteras

La carretera es una franja de tierra por donde circulan **vehículos**. Normalmente, comunica a dos ciudades. La construcción de carreteras se inició mucho antes de que se inventara el automóvil, y por ellas viajaban hace tiempo carros arrastrados por animales, llevando mercancías de un lugar a otro.

Redes de carreteras

Todas las ciudades tienen carreteras interconectadas. Esto se llama red de carreteras. Los **ingenieros** planean las redes cuidadosamente para evitar los problemas de tráfico.

▼ Las grandes ciudades están unidas por autopistas, que son grandes carreteras con varios carriles en ambas direcciones.

Cómo se construye una carretera

Las modernas se construyen en etapas. Primero, se elige el camino. Luego se quitan tierra y rocas para aplanar el terreno. Se comprime para afirmarlo y se recubre con capas de grava, concreto y mallas de alambre de acero. Después, se coloca encima una capa de concreto o de asfalto.

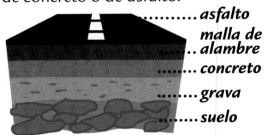

.... *asfalto*
malla de
.. *alambre*
.... *concreto*
.... *grava*
.... *suelo*

Para entrar a la autopista, los coches deben circular por una vía de salida.

El paso elevado se construye sobre otro para que el tráfico fluya con rapidez.

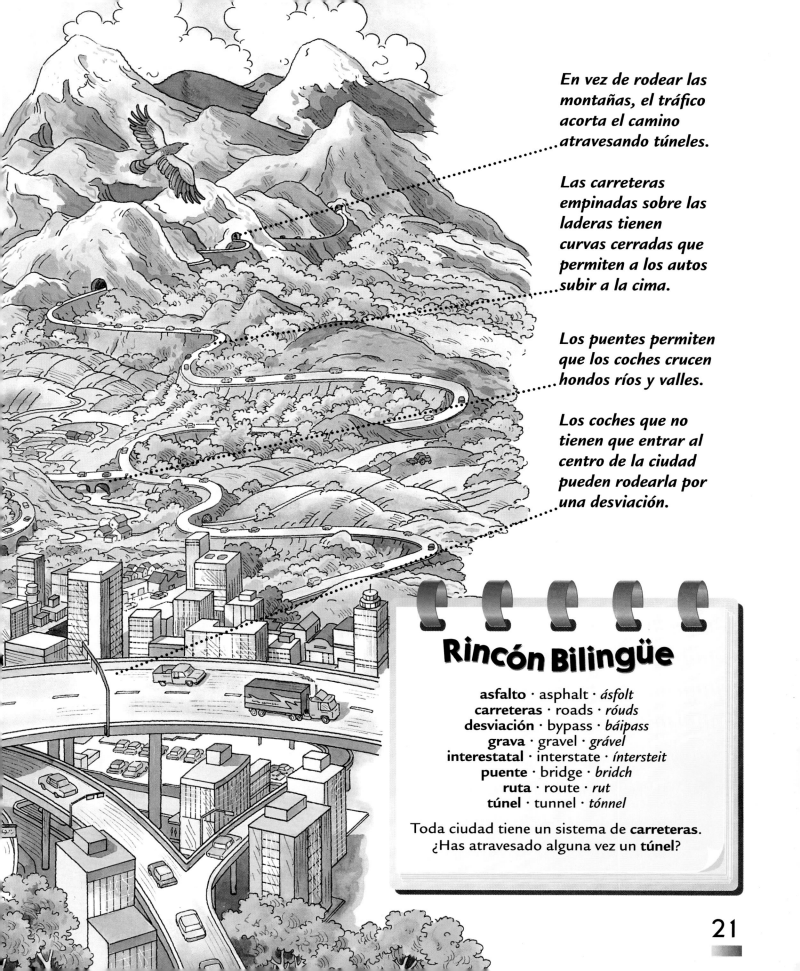

En vez de rodear las montañas, el tráfico acorta el camino atravesando túneles.

Las carreteras empinadas sobre las laderas tienen curvas cerradas que permiten a los autos subir a la cima.

Los puentes permiten que los coches crucen hondos ríos y valles.

Los coches que no tienen que entrar al centro de la ciudad pueden rodearla por una desviación.

Rincón Bilingüe

asfalto · asphalt · *ásfolt*
carreteras · roads · *róuds*
desviación · bypass · *báipass*
grava · gravel · *grável*
interestatal · interstate · *íntersteit*
puente · bridge · *bridch*
ruta · route · *rut*
túnel · tunnel · *tónnel*

Toda ciudad tiene un sistema de **carreteras**. ¿Has atravesado alguna vez un **túnel**?

véase: El metro, pág. 24

Trenes

El tren es una larga fila de vagones, arrastrados por una locomotora a lo largo de una vía. Los primeros trenes eran impulsados con vapor, pero actualmente lo son por electricidad o **diesel.** El primer ferrocarril de vapor se inauguró en 1825 y era lento, sucio e incómodo. Hoy, rápidos y limpios, los trenes eléctricos toman la electricidad de cables aéreos.

▼ Este monorraíl en Sydney, Australia, ocupa poco espacio y deja el suelo libre para que la gente camine por él.

Siempre en los rieles

Los trenes poseen ruedas especiales que les permiten mantenerse sobre los rieles. La base sobresale del borde interior de la rueda, impidiendo que el tren se salga de la vía.

base

riel

Trenes modernos

Un tipo de tren, que se llama monorraíl, circula por encima de la ciudad sobre un solo raíl. Los monorraíles son más rápidos y baratos que los trenes normales de pasajeros. Son también más silenciosos porque tienen ruedas de caucho.

Rincón Bilingüe

carga · freight · *fréit*
diesel · diesel · *díssel*
electricidad · electricity · *electríssiti*
monorraíl · monorail · *monorréil*
pasajero · passenger · *pássencher*
raíl · rail · *réil*
tren · train · *tréin*
vapor · steam · *stim*

¿Son limpios los trenes de **vapor**?
¿Qué **tren** viaja sobre un solo **raíl**?

CURIOSIDADES

El "Rocket" fue la primera máquina de vapor que se movía más rápido que un jinete a caballo. Ganó la primera carrera mundial de máquinas de vapor en 1829.

Clases de trenes

Los trenes transportan pasajeros o mercancía. Los de mercancías, o trenes de **carga**, son más largos que los de pasajeros y pueden tener más de 200 furgones.

▼ Los trenes de **carga** son excelentes para transportar por tierra las mercancías.

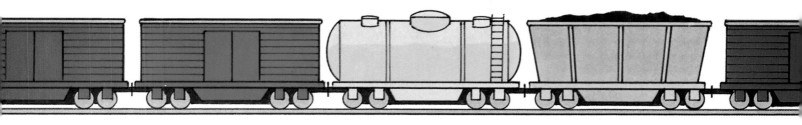

23

véase: Trenes, pág. 22

El metro

Las ciudades con mucho tráfico tienen trenes subterráneos. En las horas punta, es más rápido viajar bajo tierra. El metro transporta a un gran número de pasajeros, y no causa embotellamientos de tráfico.

CURIOSIDADES

Cuando se inauguró el metro de Londres, Inglaterra, llevaba locomotoras de vapor. ¡El humo impedía a veces ver en los túneles!

El metro en otras partes del mundo
El más viejo y largo es el de Londres, inaugurado en 1863. El que tiene más estaciones es el de Nueva York, Estados Unidos, con 469 paradas.

Los tickets se compran en máquinas o en las taquillas.

Las puertas automáticas se abren cuando metes el ticket en la ranura.

Las escaleras automáticas te llevan a los andenes.

El personal de las salas de control vigila los trenes y los andenes en las pantallas de video.

Las escaleras de emergencia se usan si las automáticas fallan.

Grandes planos en las paredes te ayudan a planear tu viaje.

Debajo de las calles de la ciudad, el metro permite que la gente se traslade.

Horas punta

Dos veces al día, en todas las ciudades del mundo, miles de personas entran y salen del trabajo. Durante esas horas punta, el metro cumple su útil cometido.

▲ En Tokio, Japón, a las horas punta los "empujadores" ayudan a meter más personas en los vagones.

El túnel del Canal de la Mancha

No sólo hay túneles debajo de las ciudades. El túnel del Canal de la Mancha, que une Inglaterra y Francia, se encuentra bajo el mar. Se inauguró en 1994 y tiene una longitud de 50 km.

Rincón Bilingüe

el **más largo** · longest · *longuest*
hora punta · rush hour · *rosh áuer*
subterráneo · underground · *ondergráund*

el **más viejo** · oldest · *óldest*   **muy activo** · busy · *bíssi*
escaleras · stairs · *stéars*   **países** · countries · *cóntris*

¿Qué **países** une el túnel del Canal de la Mancha?
El tren **subterráneo** es un buen medio de transporte.

véase: Fuerza animal, pág. 4

Viajes sobre la nieve

En las regiones heladas del Norte, como Laponia y Alaska, la tierra está casi siempre cubierta de hielo y nieve, y, por ello, se hace difícil viajar en auto o en autobús. Así, se utilizan **vehículos** diseñados para deslizarse sobre el terreno helado.

Viajes sobre el hielo y la nieve

En el pasado, se usaban los trineos para transportar personas y mercancías por las tierras heladas. Los trineos eran tirados por perros esquimales. Hoy, la gente prefiere viajar en nivimóviles, que están dotados de motor.

HAZ LA PRUEBA

Las raquetas son más anchas y planas que los zapatos normales. Esto evita que se hundan en la nieve. Corta un trozo de cartón en forma de un zapato grande y sujétalo a uno de tus pies. Así, y con el otro pie descalzo, camina por la arena. ¿Cuál de los dos pies se hunde?

▼ Este conductor de trineo les grita órdenes a sus perros. El número de perros que arrastra el trineo, depende de la **carga**.

▲ Los nivimóviles se deslizan suavemente, porque se asientan sobre dos esquíes.

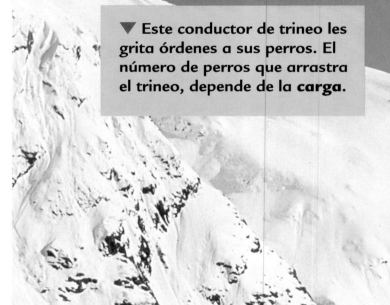

Esquiar a campo traviesa

En las regiones de nieve, como Dinamarca, Noruega o Finlandia, esquiar a campo traviesa es un medio barato y rápido de viajar. Además, es un ejercicio sano. En las Olimpíadas de invierno hay competencias de esquiar a campo traviesa.

▲ Esquiar es un deporte emocionante.

Rincón Bilingüe

esquí · ski · *squí*
frío · cold · *cóuld*
hielo · ice · *áis*
huskies (perros esquimales) · huskies · *jóskis*
nivimóvil · snowmobile · *snóumobil*
raqueta para nieve · snowshoe · *snóushu*
trineo · sled · *sled*

Los **perros esquimales** son muy fuertes.
Los **trineos** facilitan los viajes sobre el **hielo**.
¿Te gustaría subirte a un **nivimóvil**?

véase: Automóviles, pág. 10; Autobuses y tranvías, pág. 12

En el futuro

Siempre se hacen mejoras en los trenes, autobuses, autos y camiones para que sean más rápidos, seguros y cómodos. Los gases que expelen los motores dañan el ambiente; por eso, es mejor usar el transporte público en lo posible, pues ahorra gasolina y reduce la contaminación.

Energía del futuro
Mucha gente trabaja en el desarrollo de nuevos tipos de transporte, movidos por otras clases de **energía**, entre éstas la electricidad o la luz solar.

▶ Paneles especiales cambian aquí la **energía** solar en **potencia**.

▲ Este auto, diseñado en Francia, recorre grandes distancias con poquísima gasolina.

Que nada se detenga

Los nuevos sistemas de control de tráfico se diseñan para evitar los embotellamientos de **vehículos**. Con cámaras fílmicas y computadoras, la policía de tráfico detecta problemas y accidentes, para resolverlos a tiempo.

Rincón Bilingüe

accidente · accident · *ácsident*
cámara · camera · *quémera*
combustible · fuel · *fiúel*
computadora · computer · *compiúter*
contaminación · pollution · *polushon*
embotellamiento · traffic jam · *tráfic cham*
energía · energy · *énerchi*
maleta · suitcase · *súutquéis*

¡Tratemos de eliminar la **contaminación**!
El Sol es una fuente de **energía**.

▲ **Una computadora de navegación al frente del auto guía al conductor para que éste evite los embotellamientos.**

¿Qué sigue?

Los científicos no cesan de diseñar vehículos de transporte de gente y de mercancías. Estos nuevos modos de transporte, que ahora parecen extraños, no tardarán en invadir las calles de las ciudades.

▶ **Este cochecito cabe dentro de una maleta especial. Cuando no se utiliza, puede plegarse y cargarse.**

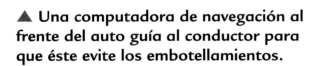

Curiosidades

● La estación de ferrocarril más grande del mundo es la Gran Estación Central de Nueva York. Está construida en dos niveles con 47 vías en el de arriba y 26 en el de abajo.

☆ *¿Sabes por qué la **potencia** de un motor se mide en caballos? Se basa en la fuerza de arrastre del caballo. El caballo de fuerza tiene la misma potencia que ese animal.*

● ¿Sabías que existe un coche que puede encoger su rueda trasera, pudiendo así estacionarse en los lugares pequeños? El nuevo concepto del Matra Zoom, de Renault, está sólo en la etapa de investigación. Todavía no está disponible.

☆ *En Italia tienen un tren diseñado para inclinarse hacia dentro cuando circula por curvas; así, el tren no tiene que aminorar su velocidad en ningún momento, lográndose tiempos de recorrido más cortos.*

● Los perros esquimales tienen una gruesa capa de pelo para conservar el calor del cuerpo. De noche, no duermen en perreras; se hacen la cama en la nieve.

☆ *El estadounidense Henry Ford fue el primero en fabricar sus coches en "línea de montaje". Mecánicos expertos montan las piezas para los coches en cada lugar distinto de la línea. Los mecánicos sólo aprenden un cometido, y, al tiempo que sólo realizan una tarea, se producen muchos coches.*

● El coche más grande del mundo tiene una alberca en la parte de atrás y también una enorme cama de agua, por si quieres echar una siesta. Esta limusina de 26 ruedas mide más de 30 m de largo y se construyó en California.

☆ *¡La ciudad de México tiene los peores embotellamientos del mundo! Tiene la flota de taxis más grande, y 60,000 peseras.*

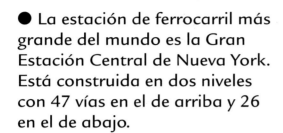

Glosario

aerodinámico Objeto sobre el cual el aire o el agua pasan fácilmente. Un auto aerodinámico reduce la fricción y es más rápido.

ambiente El mundo que nos rodea.

carga Mercancía que se traslada por tren, camión, barco, etc.

combustible Sustancia que, al quemarse, crea calor o energía. Los motores lo necesitan para funcionar.

contaminación Desechos y objetos insalubres arrojados en el ambiente.

contaminar Dañar el aire, suelo o agua con basura o sustancias nocivas.

diesel Combustible para ciertos motores.

energía Capacidad de alguien o algo para realizar un trabajo, como hacer que un motor funcione.

fricción Fuerza causada por el roce de dos superficies. Al rozar las llantas con el asfalto, la fricción frena las ruedas.

horas punta Las horas del día en que miles de personas entran y salen del trabajo.

ingeniero Aquel que diseña objetos útiles para la gente.

motor Máquina que transforma la energía en movimiento.

plataforma El suelo de un vehículo.

potencia La fuerza para realizar un trabajo.

radios Varillas delgadas que unen el centro de una rueda con su borde o aro.

rodadura Surcos y rayas en la llanta que la adhieren más al piso. Las rodaduras también repelen el agua y evitan que la llanta resbale.

ruta El camino que se sigue para llegar a un lugar determinado.

sirena Máquina que emite un sonido de alarma en un vehículo de emergencia.

vehículo El que sirve para transportar personas o artículos de un lugar a otro.

Índice

Publicado en los Estados Unidos y
Canadá por
Two-Can Publishing LLC
234 Nassau Street
Princeton, NJ 08542
con permiso de
C.D. Stampley Enterprises, Inc.

© 2002, 1997 Two-Can Publishing

Para más información sobre libros
y multimedia Two-Can, llame al
teléfono 1-609-921-6700, fax 1-609-
921-3349, o consulte nuestro sitio web
http://www.two-canpublishing.com

Texto: Deborah Chancellor
Asesor: Eryl Davies
Arte: Colin King, Stuart Trotter
Arte en computación: D. Oliver
Director editorial: Jane Wilsher
Director arte: Carole Orbell
Director producción: Lorraine Estelle
Responsable proyecto: Eljay Yildirim
Editores: Belinda Webster,
Deborah Kespert
Asistentes editoriales: Julia Hillyard,
Claire Yude
Editor co-edición: Leila Peerun
Investigación en fotografía:
Dipika Palmer-Jenkins
Traducción al español:
María Teresa Sanz

Derechos reservados. Queda prohibida
la reproducción, almacenamiento en
sistema alguno de recuperación o
transmisión en forma alguna o por
algún medio electrónico, mecánico,
de fotocopiado, grabación, o cualquier
otra forma, de cualquier parte de esta
publicación, sin previa autorización
del propietario de los derechos.

HC ISBN 1-58728-646-7
SC ISBN 1-58728-703-X

HC 1 2 3 4 5 6 7 8 9 10 05 04 03
SC 1 2 3 4 5 6 7 8 9 10 05 04 03

Créditos fotográficos: Britstock-IFA
p15sd, p27si; Colorific p26ii;
Hutchison Library (H.R. Dorig) p4sd;
Image Bank p14ii, p17si, p19sd;
A.C. Press p29id; Quadrant p14ic;
Spectrum p5; Tony Stone Images
cubierta, p8i, p22-23c, p25sd;
Frank Spooner p28i&s, p29si;
Telegraph Colour Library p18ii; Zefa
p6ii, p7cd, p9, p11s, p12, p26-27ic.

Impreso en Hong Kong

HISTORIC
COMMUNITIES

TRAVEL
in the Early Days

Bobbie Kalman and Kate Calder

Crabtree Publishing Company

www.crabtreebooks.com

386
KAI
C.1
a 15.45
2003

HISTORIC COMMUNITIES

Created by Bobbie Kalman

To Heather Levigne
from across the hall

Editor-in-Chief
Bobbie Kalman

Writing team
Bobbie Kalman
Kate Calder

Managing editor
Lynda Hale

Editors
Niki Walker
Hannelore Sotzek
John Crossingham
Amanda Bishop

Computer design
Lynda Hale

Production coordinator
Hannelore Sotzek

Special thanks to
Black Creek Pioneer Village / TRCA

Photographs
Black Creek Pioneer Village / TRCA: pages 10 (both), 11 (all)

Illustrations and reproductions
Valérie Apprioual: pages 3 (teamboat), 6 (middle and bottom), 7 (bottom); Barbara Bedell: cover (inset), title page, pages 3 (all except boats), 8, 12-13, 16, 17, 22, 23 (top), 25, 26 (bottom), 27, 28, 29, 30; Antoinette "Cookie" Bortolon: page 6 (top); ©Crabtree Publishing Company: pages 26, 31 (bottom); Currier & Ives: page 24; John Mantha: back cover; Jeannette McNaughton-Julich: page 31 (top); Janet Newey: page 9 (bottom); Bonna Rouse: pages 3 (keelboat), 5 (bottom), 7 (top and middle), 9 (top), 12 (top), 14, 15, 19; other images by Digital Stock and Eyewire, Inc.

Digital prepress
Best Graphics Int'l Co.; Embassy Graphics (cover)

Printer
Worzalla Publishing Company

Crabtree Publishing Company

www.crabtreebooks.com   1-800-387-7650

PMB 16A
350 Fifth Ave.,
Suite 3308
New York, NY
10118

612 Welland Ave.
St. Catharines,
Ontario,
Canada
L2M 5V6

73 Lime Walk
Headington
Oxford
0X3 7AD
United Kingdom

Copyright © **2001 CRABTREE PUBLISHING COMPANY**.
All rights reserved. No part of this publication may be reproduced, stored in a retrieval system or be transmitted in any form or by any means, electronic, mechanical, photocopying, recording, or otherwise, without the prior written permission of Crabtree Publishing Company.

Cataloging-in-Publication Data
Kalman, Bobbie
    Travel in the early days

p. cm. — (Historic communities)
Includes index.

ISBN 0-86505-442-8 (library bound) — ISBN 0-86505-472-X (pbk.)
This book introduces readers to transportation used by settlers in North America. Topics include covered wagons, canal boats, steam power, and hazards that early travelers faced.

1. Transportation—North America—History—Juvenile literature.
[1. Transportation—History.] I. Calder, Kate. II. Title. III. Series: Kalman, Bobbie. Historic communities.

HE151 .K323 2001   j388' .0973—dc21   LC00-034609
                                                                              CIP

Contents

Travel in a new land

Modern travel is quick and simple. Roads, cars, trains, and airplanes make it easy to get from place to place. In the past, however, travel was slow, difficult, and often dangerous. When the first explorers reached North America, they faced rough land, thick forests, and raging rivers. These adventurers did not journey far from major waterways such as rivers and lakes.

Canoe travel

About two hundred years after the first explorers arrived, the fur trade was thriving in North America. Hundreds of traders came in search of wealth. They traded with the Native Americans, who traveled in small, lightweight boats called **canoes**. Trappers and fur traders quickly adopted this important means of travel. Now they could travel deep inland along shallow rivers and streams where larger boats could not go. Some canoes were big enough to transport sixty people as well as supplies, equipment, and furs. Smaller canoes could be **portaged**, or lifted and carried across land from one waterway to another.

Over land

On land, the first settlers followed trails made by Native Americans. Travelers also **blazed** trails of their own. Blazed trails were marked by cuts made in trees with a **hatchet**. These trails kept people from getting lost. Marked trails also connected settlements that developed inland. Most new settlers traveled on foot and walked many miles over rough, forested land to reach the next town. Wild animals made the journey even more threatening.

No bridges

Explorers traveling inland were unaware of all the rivers and lakes that crisscrossed the land. Many travelers came across large bodies of water. There were no bridges, so they often had to walk for hours to find a shallow spot where they could wade across. Some people made temporary bridges by laying long tree trunks across rivers.

(top) Native Americans showed hunters and trappers how to build birch-bark canoes.

(right) In the winter, hunters and trappers trudged through the deep snow with snowshoes, which kept them from sinking.

Dugouts *were boats made from large tree trunks. The trunks were hollowed out and chiseled to form a canoe.*

On the water

Waterways were crucial to the early settlers because shipments of supplies from Europe arrived by boat. Settlements and farms were established along rivers and lakes so that people, tools, food, and other goods could be transported easily from place to place. Settlers built a variety of boats for traveling on lakes and rivers. They used paddles, sails, poles, and horses to move the boats through water.

Bateaux

Bateaux were long narrow boats with large sails. When there was no wind to fill the sails and move the bateau, passengers had to push the boat along with poles or paddles. Trappers and traders transported their furs to towns and cities by bateaux. Many settler families also traveled on these boats. When night fell, the boat was **docked**, or tied to shore. The passengers camped nearby or slept at a hotel if there was one in the area.

bateau

flatboat

Flatboats

Flatboats were large, wide boats with a flat bottom for traveling on shallow rivers. They used the river's **current**, or flow, to float along. A large oar at the back of the boat steered it left or right. People stored their belongings in the cabin, which also provided a place to sleep and eat. Some families lived on their flatboat for months while they traveled down a river. When they arrived at the site of their new home, they used the boat as their temporary shelter until they could build a house.

keelboat

Keelboats

Keelboats were long boats with points at both the front and back. Settlers used these boats to travel upstream against the current. A large **keel** ran along the bottom of the boat. It protected the **hull** against logs or rocks that were under water. Keelboats had a sail to power the boat with wind. If there was no wind, the passengers pushed the boat using poles. They walked on the deck along wooden rungs, which allowed them to dig in their heels for extra pushing power. Often one passenger played a fiddle while the others pushed to the beat of the music.

Canal boats

Artificial waterways known as **canals** were constructed for traveling in areas where rivers were too rough for travel or where rivers did not flow. **Canal boats** were long boats that had a large, flat-topped cabin. Some of the passengers sat on top of the cabin as the boat moved along the canal. Mules or horses were attached by a rope and pulled the boat along from the shore. Sometimes several families lived on a canal boat while they traveled to their new home.

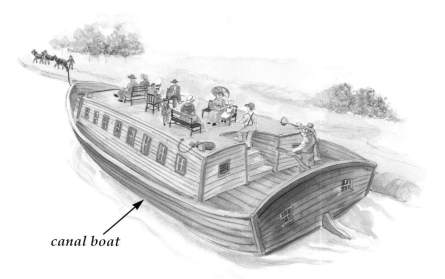

canal boat

Horse power

Teamboats used horses to move the boat forward. The horses were placed in booths on each side of the boat. When the horses walked, they caused a large wheel under the deck to turn. The wheel was attached to an **axle**, which turned paddles. The paddles pushed the boat through the water. Most teamboats were used as **ferries** to carry people across rivers. Without bridges, ferries were the only way settlers could cross some deep, wide rivers.

teamboat

Roads and wagons

Some settlers brought horses and oxen with them from Europe to North America. These animals were bred by the settlers and became plentiful in the new land. The settlers depended on horses and oxen to transport them and their belongings from place to place. These animals were also used in the fields to clear the land and plant and harvest crops.

Important animals

Animals were very valuable to the settlers. If a horse or ox was stolen, settlers were often left stranded and were unable to move heavy loads. In many places it was a serious crime to steal horses, and thieves were often hanged.

Wagons, carts, and carriages

Settlers also used carts and wagons to travel and to transport supplies. Simple carts were made of wooden boxes attached to wheels. Wagons were larger than carts and were used to carry people as well as supplies. Often two or more animals pulled a wagon. Horse-drawn carriages were lighter and fancier than wagons. A seat in a carriage was more comfortable because it was used only for carrying people.

Animals were attached with long poles to carts, wagons, and carriages. This settler uses his oxen to carry heavy loads. He steers them as they pull a cart full of logs for firewood.

Bumpy roads

Eventually, most of the land along waterways was settled, so new settlers had to establish their farms farther inland. The foot trails leading inland were too narrow for wagons. Over time, settlers widened these trails by cutting down the trees on either side. The trails easily became rutted and muddy with constant travel. To solve this problem, settlers split logs and laid them across the path to make a **corduroy road**. Corduroy roads were very bumpy. Horses often hurt their legs when their hoofs slipped between the logs.

Toll roads

After a **sawmill** was built in an area, people began making roads with flat boards called **planks**. Plank roads were much smoother than corduroy roads. In some places, the roads were built by companies. The company that owned the road charged people a **toll**, or fee, for traveling on it. Tollgate keepers were hired to collect fees from travelers. The fees were supposed to be used for repairing the road, but many roads were in poor condition.

(above) Corduroy roads kept settlers from getting stuck in the mud, but they made traveling bumpy and uncomfortable.

This couple has stopped at the tollgate to pay their fee, but many travelers tried to race past the toll collector without paying.

Travel tradespeople

Most settlers used their wagon or cart for both transportation and hauling goods to and from town. Very few people had the skills needed to make or repair their vehicles, so tradespeople such as blacksmiths, **farriers**, and **wheelwrights** set up workshops in towns. Settlers paid these artisans to fix broken wagons and make the supplies used for traveling.

The blacksmith

Horses, oxen, and mules needed metal shoes to protect the bottom of their hoofs. The blacksmith made U-shaped horseshoes out of iron. He heated a piece of iron in a large brick fireplace called a **forge** until the black metal turned white or yellow. The hot iron was easily cut and shaped with a hammer. The blacksmith then dipped the hot shoe into a barrel of water to cool and harden.

The harness maker

Settlers needed harnesses and straps to attach animals to wagons and control their movements. The harness maker was a skilled leather worker who sold new saddles and harnesses. He or she also repaired damaged equipment.

The farrier

A farrier **shod**, or attached, horseshoes to a horse's hoofs. He first removed damaged or worn-out horseshoes. Next, he used metal tools to clean dirt from the bottom of the hoofs. Then he filed the hoofs smooth so the shoes would fit snugly. Finally, the farrier hammered the shoes directly onto the bottom of the hoofs. He used small nails, which did not hurt the animals. Many farriers also treated wounded and diseased horses.

The blacksmith heated iron white-hot in order to shape it into horseshoes.

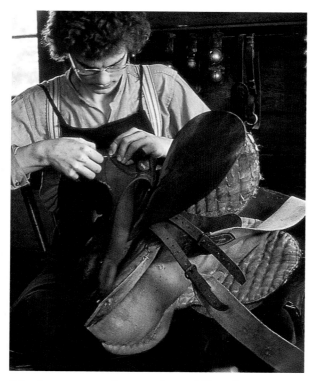

The harness maker made saddles, harnesses, and whips out of leather.

The wheelwright made and repaired wheels. The first wagon wheels were made entirely of wood. In later times, the wheelwright attached metal tires to the rims to make the wheels last longer.

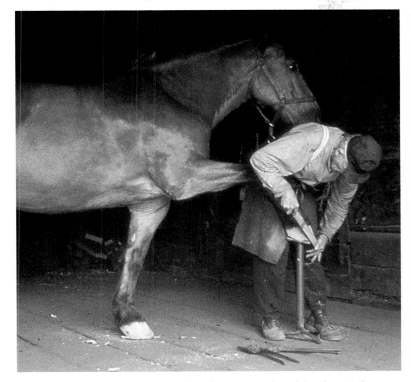

Some blacksmiths were also farriers. This blacksmith files the horse's hoofs to keep them healthy and strong.

*The **wainwright** made wagons and carriages for the townspeople.*

Gliding over snow

When winter arrived, the harsh, cold weather required changes in the modes of transportation. Deep snow on the trails made walking impossible, and wagon wheels often got stuck. Water froze, so people could not travel by boat on rivers and lakes. To cope with winter, settlers found new ways to get around on ice and snow.

Traveling on foot

Some settlers used snowshoes to walk on snow. Others strapped long strips of wood to their boots. Settlers used these "skis" to glide over the snow. They pushed themselves along with long poles.

Sleighs

Instead of wagons and carts, people traveled in **sleighs** in the winter. Sleighs were similar to carts, but they had no wheels. Two flat metal bars called **runners** slid easily over snow. Sleighs came in different shapes and sizes. Some were plain wagons, but others were fancy. **Cutters** were small sleighs that were pulled by a single horse. Some settlers traveled on a small sled pulled by a team of dogs.

Snowshoes were wide wooden frames with leather netting. They were strapped onto boots.

Rivers and lakes were not an obstacle in winter. The thick ice made it easy for travelers to glide over them. This winter stagecoach has runners instead of wheels.

Time for fun

During the winter months, people finally had some free time to enjoy themselves. The settlers did not have to tend their crops, and autumn chores such as preserving food and grinding grain were completed. They used this opportunity to visit friends, especially during the Christmas holiday season. To make their sleighs more festive, people attached bells and ribbons to the bridles of their horses. The bells acted as a signal to other travelers that a sleigh was coming. The expression, "I'll be there with bells on" means "I'm looking forward to visiting you!"

*(above) People kept warm on a sleigh by covering themselves with fur blankets. Sometimes they put **foot warmers** on the floor. Foot warmers were metal boxes filled with hot coals.*

Winter hazards

Winter travel was usually comfortable and quick. Gliding over snow was a happy change from bumpy rides in wagons and coaches. Sleighs slid smoothly over stumps, ruts, and rocks that lay buried deep under snow. Snow travel could be risky, however. Speedy drivers often lost control of their sleigh. Large, steep snowdrifts also caused sleighs to overturn or get stuck.

Blizzards

Blizzards were a winter traveler's greatest fear. People who were outdoors during a blizzard could quickly freeze to death. Travelers caught in sudden snowstorms sometimes lost their way and became stranded. They could do little but huddle together with their animals for warmth while waiting for the storm to end.

Feeling the way

Thick snow and driving wind could be so blinding that settlers sometimes got lost on their own farm! To find their way in snowstorms, people tied a rope between their house and barn. During blizzards, they held onto the rope and used it to guide them from one building to another.

On thin ice

Traveling over ice that was not frozen solid was extremely dangerous. Large areas of thin ice were often hidden under a fresh blanket of snow. If the ice cracked and broke, the driver had to act quickly. He or she tied a rope around the horse's neck to keep the animal's head above water and then pulled on the rope to help the horse to safety.

These settlers have had a freezing surprise. Their sleigh was too heavy for the ice.

Stagecoaches

In the mid-1700s, **stagecoaches** were a common mode of transportation. Stagecoaches were carriages that took people from town to town. Travelers were charged a fee according to how far they were traveling. At some stops the driver changed horses. These carriages were called stagecoaches because the distance between stops was known as a **stage** of the journey.

This village has stables for sheltering horses. There is a tavern where people can buy a meal or spend the night while the stagecoach stops to change horses. Which jobs are being done by the coachmen at this stage stop? Examine the picture and name four tasks.

Tough going

Many stagecoaches were uncomfortable. They were small, cramped, and provided a bumpy ride. Passengers sat inside the carriage, on the front bench with the driver, or even on top of the coach. Stagecoaches were unsteady on the rough roads and sometimes tipped over. Passengers often had to lean to one side to make sure the coach stayed upright!

Dangerous drivers

A stagecoach driver was known as a **coachman**. Some coachmen were reckless drivers who tried to reach the next town as quickly as possible. The faster they finished a trip, the sooner they could start another one and make more money. They turned corners sharply and sped along dangerously with little care for the comfort or safety of their passengers.

Mail carriers

Some stagecoaches carried mail as well as passengers. Every week, mail was collected from and delivered to general stores along the stagecoach route. Bandits often robbed stagecoaches that carried mail because many letters contained money.

This stagecoach is caught in a winter storm. Riding on top of the cabin is cold, but the coachman continues to forge ahead.

This stagecoach is heading out of town on a Sunday sightseeing trip. In the summer, sightseeing trips were a popular pastime.

17

Wagon trains

In the mid-1800s, many settlers left eastern towns and cities to seek new opportunities in the West. They began their long journey in April or May and took several months to reach their destination. Harsh weather, wild animals, fast-flowing rivers, and steep, rocky mountain passes made the trip difficult and dangerous. There was also the risk of injury and disease. Settlers traveled in a long **convoy**, or group, of many wagons known as a **wagon train**. Being in a wagon train provided protection and support for the long journey.

Covered wagons

Settlers transported their possessions in a **covered wagon**. They stretched a canvas **tarpaulin**, or cover, over a wooden frame to protect the contents of the wagon. Early covered wagons were called **Conestoga wagons**. They were used for transporting supplies and traveling between towns. As people started traveling great distances to the West, they built covered wagons that were bigger and sturdier for the long distances across the plains and mountains.

Prairie schooners

The settlers called the covered wagons **prairie schooners** after a type of sailing ship called a **schooner**. From a distance, a wagon's white cover looked like a ship's sail. Large wheels lifted the wagon high off the ground so it would not hit rocks or stumps along the path. The distance between the wagon and the ground also helped when crossing a river. If the water was too deep, the settlers removed the wheels and floated the wagon across the river like a raft.

No free rides

The wagon was fully packed with the family's supplies which made it very heavy. The driver sat on a bench at the front of the wagon, and others walked alongside to make it easier for the animals to pull. Only small children or sick family members rode inside.

Wagon trains traveled through all types of harsh weather, including thunderstorms. The travelers could not afford to stop, even in very stormy weather. They had a long way to go and wanted to complete the trip before winter. They did not want to be caught in a deadly blizzard!

Western travel

Most of the West was unsettled wilderness with no roads. Horses were essential for travel and work in the West. Many people mined for gold or worked on cattle ranches. Miners relied on horses to carry supplies long distances. Cowboys rode horses to round up cattle and **drive**, or guide, them to market. Horses were also needed to pull stagecoaches carrying travelers.

Western coaches

Traveling west in a stagecoach was tiring. Passengers often rode all night through the vast wilderness. The few hotels along the trail were uncomfortable and dirty. They had thin walls made of canvas, and travelers slept on mattresses of flour sacks stuffed with straw. Coaches stopped for short breaks at **ranchos**, which were small taverns with dirt floors.

Stagecoaches in the West were even less comfortable than those in the East. Western passengers faced long and difficult journeys over rough, dusty trails.

*Before ranchers and miners began settling in the West, herds of wild horses roamed the land. Mexican cowboys, called **vaqueros**, caught many of these wild horses and tamed them. They taught the cowboys from the eastern towns how to tame horses and herd and rope cattle.*

The Wild West

Many criminals moved west because there were few sheriffs. Criminals made travel difficult and even dangerous. Travelers feared attacks from bandits on the long, lonely trails. Thieves often stole settlers' possessions such as clothing, tools, money, and even their horses! This lawless land became known as the "Wild West."

Traveling on horseback was the cheapest and quickest way to travel. The horses became accustomed to walking over the steep, rocky land in mountainous areas and on the hot, dry sand in the deserts.

Traveling by stagecoach was risky. Outlaws often stopped coaches along the trails and robbed the passengers of their money and jewelry.

*Western women did not ride **sidesaddle**, as women riders did in the East. They straddled the horse, making riding much easier.*

In the city

As cities grew, the sidewalks became crowded with people and the streets bustled with wagons, carriages, and stagecoaches. Sometimes the streets were so crowded with traffic that it was difficult to get anywhere! Streetcars and bicycles were common modes of transportation in the city.

The tires of penny farthings were made of metal hoops, which were easily bent and damaged by ruts or rocks on the road.

Bicycles

Many people began riding bicycles in the late 1800s. Riding a bicycle was quicker than walking and did not require a horse. The first bicycles were called **penny farthings**. They had a huge front wheel on which the seat was placed, making it difficult to get on and off. Eventually, penny farthings were replaced by bicycles with two even-sized wheels.

*The **hansom cab** was named after its designer, Joseph Hansom. The passengers of this carriage gave instructions to the driver through a trap door in the roof.*

Large wooden carriages carried passengers through the city streets.

Streetcars

Early streetcars were large coaches pulled by horses. Later streetcars traveled along metal tracks that were built into the roads. They were pulled by a team of horses or mules. The cars had a roof, but often the sides had open windows, so the passengers got wet and cold when it rained or snowed. Passengers paid a small fee to ride the streetcars. The driver stopped to pick up passengers at any point along the route. To request a stop, they signaled the driver by pulling on a string that was attached to his foot.

Sometimes a streetcar ran off the tracks. In order to continue on their journey, the passengers had to get out and help put the car back on the tracks.

Sunday drivers

On Sundays, many people dressed in their finest clothes and took carriage rides through the city. The horses were well-groomed, and the carriages were polished and shiny. Sunday drives allowed people to show off their best clothes, horses, and carriages.

Those who could not afford to own a fine team of horses or a shiny carriage, such as the one in this picture, watched those who could. This handsome couple is getting a lot of attention! People stop and stare, wishing they could ride in such a fine carriage and wear such beautiful clothes.

Steam power

The invention of the steam engine changed the way people traveled. In the early 1800s, steam engines were designed to power boats and trains. A steam engine is fueled by burning coal or wood. The heat from this fire boils water, creating steam. The steam builds up in a closed container and creates a lot of pressure. When the steam is released from the container, its force moves wheels inside the engine. As these wheels turn, they also force the wheels of the vehicle to turn.

Steam engines allowed people to travel faster and easier than ever before. The steamboats in this picture had a paddle wheel on either side of the boat. Others had a single paddle wheel at the back.

The first steamboats

Steamboats used steam engines to turn giant paddle wheels, which pushed the boats through water. Some steamboats had sails so they could also use the wind for power. The first steamboats were unstable and uncomfortable. The bouncy, rocking motion of the boat made many passengers ill. Steamboat captains also enjoyed racing them against other boats, adding to the passengers' rough ride. Racing could overheat the engine and create too much steam, causing the engine to explode.

Popular way to travel

Soon, bigger and better steamboats were built. They were safer and much more comfortable for long journeys. Steamboats became a popular means of travel and were used to ship goods such as sugar, cattle, and cotton to various cities.

Many steamboats were luxurious. They had beautiful furniture, carpeting, and fine china. Musicians were often hired to entertain the guests. Some steamboats even had a casino on board where people could gamble.

The railroad

In the early locomotives, water boiled to steam in metal pipes. The pipes were heated by a wood fire in a firebox. The pressure from the steam moved a piston back and forth, which turned the wheels.

Steam engines called **locomotives** pulled trains. The building of the first locomotives was part of an experiment in the early 1800s. People wanted to see if a cart could be powered by a steam engine. Before long, people built locomotives with cars for carrying passengers and goods. The first railroads linked large eastern cities. This new and fast method of travel became popular, and railway tracks soon spread westward. In later years, many people traveled by rail to settle new areas all over North America.

Building the railroad

Building railroads was slow, backbreaking work. Thousands of workers laid logs called **ties** on the ground. Heavy iron rails were then laid on the ties. Finally, long spikes were pounded into the ties to hold the rails in place. When the track had to pass through a mountain, dynamite was used to blast a hole through the rock. Many men risked their lives by blasting rock to create tunnels and passageways for the railroad.

The first steam-powered locomotive was made in England in 1804.

Linking East and West

In 1869, a cross-country railway was completed. It linked towns and cities across the United States from east to west. By 1885, Canada also had a cross-country railroad. Traveling by transcontinental railways was faster, safer, and more comfortable than making the trip in a wagon.

This 1831 locomotive was one of the first to be built in North America.

Settling new areas

The railroad played an important role in settling the western regions of both the United States and Canada. It took months to get from the east to the west by wagon, but by train it took only days. More and more people left their home in the East to start a new life in the West, where cheap land was available. People also came from other countries and made the difficult journey to these western areas.

Made in 1900, this locomotive had a cab for the engineer. It was one of the first engines to burn coal instead of wood.

Passenger trains

Early train cars were simple wooden carts with iron wheels, and the passenger cars resembled stagecoaches. As trains became more popular, bigger and better cars were built so passengers could travel more comfortably. Depending on how much they could afford, travelers chose seats in third-class, second-class, or first-class cars.

Tickets for the third-class cars were the least expensive. Passengers rested on wooden benches and bunks. There were no dining or sleeping cars in third class. Passengers ate food they had packed for the trip. Most of the passengers were people moving west to start a new life. They could not afford to pay for the more expensive tickets.

Second class

Second-class cars had cushioned seats. People could sleep in their seats or in bunks. If they paid extra, they could sleep in a separate sleeping car. Some second-class passengers brought their own food. Others got off the train to have a meal in a restaurant when the train stopped at a station to refuel.

First class

First-class tickets were the most expensive. The luxurious first-class cars had large cushioned seats. On long trips, travelers slept in sleeping cars with private beds. They ate in a dining car that served delicious meals on fine china. For first-class passengers, such as those shown below, riding the train was like taking a vacation.

Turn-of-the-century travel

As the population of towns and cities grew, new and improved roads were built. The invention of steamboats and trains made travel easier and more enjoyable. Traveling from town to town or even across the continent would soon become even faster. Which new modes of transportation did the 1900s have in store?

The first flyers

After land and water travel were no longer a challenge, people looked to the sky for faster ways of getting from place to place. The first flyers were inventors who patterned their machines after birds. To make these devices fly, they jumped off high places and hoped that their flying machines would keep them in the air. Unfortunately, most of these brave inventors experienced crash landings!

Balloons

Hot-air balloons were the first flying machines that carried people across the sky. People knew that hot air rises, so they used a flame to heat the air inside a giant balloon. Up it went, lifting a large basket that carried people inside.

Look at these early flying devices. Which one do you think had the best chance of staying in the air? If you had to invent a new way to travel, what would it be? Draw a picture of your invention.

hot-air balloon

The first cars

At the end of the 1800s, people continued to invent new ways to travel. People started riding in motor carriages, which were powered by steam engines rather than horses. These early automobiles traveled slowly and used coal for fuel. Eventually, faster engines were built, which used gasoline instead of coal.

*Many people have come to see the amazing new flying machines at this fair in the early 1900s. The blimp in the right corner of the large picture is filled with a light gas called **hydrogen**, which keeps it afloat. People are excited about the airplane that just took off. On the ground, there are some early automobiles alongside a reliable horse and carriage.*

Glossary

artisan A skilled tradesperson such as a blacksmith or carpenter

axle A shaft that rotates and, in turn, rotates a wheel that is attached to it

blaze To mark a trail by cutting trees

canal An artificial waterway dug across land through which boats can travel

convoy A large group traveling together for safety and protection

current The natural flow of a body of water that moves along a path

dugout A canoe made by hollowing out a large log

forge A fireplace in which a blacksmith heats metal

hatchet A small, short-handled ax

hull The frame of a boat

keel A long piece of wood that runs underneath a boat from the front to the rear

locomotive A steam-powered engine used to push or pull train cars

piston A solid cylinder that, using pressure created by steam or liquid, moves back and forth inside a hollow cylinder

plank A long, thick, flat piece of wood cut from a log

portage To carry a canoe over land to get from one body of water to another

runners The long metal blades of a sleigh that glide over the snow

sawmill A building where logs are sawed into planks

tarpaulin Waterproof material used to cover objects and keep them dry

ties Beams of wood that are laid across railway rails to secure them in place

wagon train A group of families traveling across a great distance in covered wagons

Index

1 2 3 4 5 6 7 8 9 0   Printed in U.S.A.   9 8 7 6 5 4 3 2 1 0